Character Education:
Fostering Creativity and Problem-Solving

Copyright © 2023 by Mel Arat

All rights reserved. No part of this publication may be reproduced, distributed, or transmitted in any form or by any means, including photocopying, recording, or other electronic or mechanical methods, without the prior written permission of the publisher, except in the case of brief quotations embodied in critical reviews and certain other noncommercial uses permitted by copyright law. For permission requests, write to the publisher, addressed "Attention: Permissions Coordinator," at the address below.

New York City Books
www.nycitybooks.com

217 Peace Pipe Way
Georgetown TX 78628 USA

Printed in the United States of America

Publisher's Cataloging-in-Publication data
Arat, Mel
Character Education: Fostering Creativity and Problem-Solving

I-ISBN: 978-1-0881-2595-3
EBook-ISBN: 978-1-0881-2601-1

LCCN: 2023908607

Character Education:
Fostering Creativity and Problem-Solving

Mel ARAT

New York City Books

As a school principal, I wholeheartedly endorse "Character Education: Creativity and Problem Solving" for children, as it skillfully integrates storytelling and practical exercises to empower students with problem-solving skills and emotional intelligence, fostering well-rounded individuals ready to thrive in life.
Zeynep Yurttas, School Principal

"Character Education: Creativity and Problem Solving" is a must-read for children, combining engaging stories and practical exercises to nurture creativity and critical thinking while emphasizing essential character development for a changing world.
Hayri Koc, Student Coach

Imagination's Flight

In a world of wonder, where children play,
Their minds ablaze, in a creative array,
With imaginations soaring, they take flight,
As problem solvers, they see the light.

With colors splashed on canvas bright,
They paint a world of pure delight,
A masterpiece born from the heart,
Their creativity, a work of art.

In science, they ask, "Why?" and "How?"
With curiosity, they make us proud,
Experimenting, they boldly seek,
Unlocking mysteries, day by week.

In friendships formed, they learn to share,
Supporting each other, showing they care,
With empathy and kindness, they stand tall,
Solving conflicts, one and all.

Their minds, a playground, where ideas roam,
Creativity and problem-solving find a home,
In every child's heart, the seeds reside,
Growing bright, as they journey with pride.

So let us nurture their spirits free,
To explore, to create, to problem-solve with glee,
For in the young minds, we hold the key,
To a world of possibilities, where greatness will be.

CONTENTS

Introduction *9*

Chapter 1 Creativity and Problem Solving *13*
   Assist, Create, and Shine 14
   Study Questions 16
   Guide to Creativity and Problem Solving 17

Chapter 2 Being Solution Oriented *19*
   Soccer Game 20
   Study Questions 23
   Guide to Being solution oriented 24

Chapter 3 Critical Thinking and Questioning *27*
   Lost Pencils 28
   Study Questions: 30
   Guide to Critical Thinking and Questioning 31

Chapter 4 Developing Alternatives *33*
   Connecting Papers 34
   Study Questions 37
   Guide to Developing Alternatives 38

Chapter 5 Constructive Criticism *39*
   Yellow Flower 40
   Study Questions 43
   Guide to Constructive Criticism and Destructive Criticism:
   Understanding the Difference 44

Chapter 6 Logical Reasoning *47*
   How Do I Get to School? 48
   Study Questions: 51

Chapter 7 Solving problems using information instead of violence *53*

Bully's Redemption	54
Study Questions	57
Guide to Solving problems using information	58

Chapter 8 Being Independent — *61*

Courage to be a Lone Wolf	62
Study Questions	64
Guide to Being Independent	65

Chapter 9 Power of Humor — *67*

Fish Tales	68
Study Questions:	70
Guide to Power of Humor	71

Chapter 10 Curiosity — *73*

White hair	74
Study Questions	78
Guide to Curiosity	79

Conclusion — *81*

Introduction

This book aims to provide insight and guidance on important character traits that are crucial for personal and professional success. Each chapter explores a specific concept, ranging from Creativity and Problem Solving to Being Independent and Power of Humor. Through engaging stories and thought-provoking study questions, readers will have the opportunity to reflect on their own beliefs and attitudes, and develop the skills necessary to achieve their goals. Whether you are a student, a professional, or anyone looking to strengthen your character, this book is a valuable resource for anyone seeking personal growth and development.

Creativity and problem solving are important parts of character education because they help individuals develop the ability to think critically, adapt to new situations, and overcome challenges. These skills are essential for personal and professional success, as they enable individuals to come up with innovative solutions and approach problems in a proactive manner. In today's rapidly changing world, creativity and problem solving are more important than ever, as individuals face an ever-increasing number of complex challenges in their personal and professional lives. By teaching individuals how to be creative and effective problem solvers, character education can help individuals develop the skills they need to succeed in an increasingly dynamic and unpredictable world.

The use of fictional stories to illustrate the concepts in each chapter provides a valuable benefit to readers. These stories provide a relatable context for readers to understand the practical application of each concept. They offer a clear example of how the concept can be used in real-life situations and help readers to visualize the potential outcomes of using these skills. By providing a narrative, the stories can engage readers emotionally, making the lessons more memorable and enjoyable. The use of stories also encourages readers to think critically and develop their own solutions to problems presented in the story. Ultimately, the use of fictional stories allows readers to see the value of the concepts in action and empowers them to apply these skills in their own lives.

At the end of each story in "Character Education: Creativity and Problem Solving," there are study questions that will help the readers to deepen their understanding of the chapter concepts. The questions are designed to promote critical thinking and analysis, and to encourage readers to apply the chapter's ideas to real-life situations. By discussing and answering the study questions, readers will have the opportunity to reflect on the story and explore their own thoughts and feelings about the concepts presented in the chapter. Additionally, these questions will enable readers to engage in meaningful conversations with others and develop their communication skills. Overall, the study questions are a valuable tool that will help readers gain a deeper appreciation of the concepts presented in the book and apply them to their own lives.

Creativity and Problem Solving: Creativity is the ability to come up with new ideas, perspectives or ways of doing things, and problem-solving is the process of finding solutions to complex issues. The book delves into how developing creativity and problem-solving skills can help individuals overcome obstacles and achieve success in both personal and professional life.

Being Solution Oriented: This chapter discusses the importance of being solution-oriented in life. It encourages readers to focus on solutions rather than problems and to adopt a proactive approach to dealing with challenges.

Critical Thinking and Questioning: This chapter covers the skill of critical thinking and the value of asking questions in order to gain a deeper understanding of a situation. It explores how critical thinking can be used to evaluate information, solve problems, and make sound decisions.

Developing Alternatives: This chapter provides insights into how to develop alternative solutions to problems. It encourages readers to think creatively and to consider different options before making decisions. This chapter also highlights the benefits of having multiple solutions to a problem.

Constructive Criticism: This chapter explains how to provide and receive constructive criticism in a way that helps individuals grow and develop. It explores the importance of giving feedback in a positive manner and how to effectively address any areas of improvement.

Logical Reasoning: This chapter discusses the skill of logical reasoning and how to use it to make sound decisions. It highlights the importance of identifying and evaluating evidence, as well as making connections between different pieces of information to reach logical conclusions.

Solving problems using information: This chapter delves into the importance of gathering and analyzing information to solve problems. It covers the process of identifying and evaluating sources of information, as well as how to use data to make informed decisions.

Being Independent: This chapter encourages readers to develop independence in their thinking and decision-making. It explores the importance of taking responsibility for one's own life and decisions, as well as the benefits of being self-sufficient.

Power of Humor: This chapter highlights the power of humor in diffusing tense situations, building relationships, and reducing stress. It explores the benefits of incorporating humor in one's life and how to use it effectively.

Curiosity: This chapter covers the importance of curiosity in learning, problem-solving, and personal growth. It encourages readers to be curious about the world around them and to ask questions in order to gain new insights and knowledge.

In conclusion, "Character Education: Creativity and Problem Solving" is a valuable resource for children seeking personal growth and development. Each chapter provides valuable insights into important character traits, ranging from problem-solving and creativity to humor and curiosity. Through engaging stories and thought-provoking study questions, readers will have the opportunity to reflect on their own beliefs and attitudes, and develop the skills necessary to achieve their goals.

Chapter 1 Creativity and Problem Solving

Assist, Create, and Shine

In the not-so-glamorous, dimly lit section behind the bustling hall of the Thompson Elementary School, a throng of anxious students were preparing for the end-of-year performance. Each student was supplied with a cloak, a relic from the annual "Cloak & Dagger Extravaganza." But these weren't ordinary cloaks; they were the capes of destiny, filled with the magical power to make children trip on stairs!

When Alex, the most enthusiastic yet clumsy student, entered the hall, he hastily donned his cloak. Dashing outside, he tripped over the iron part of the stairs. His cloak, as if possessed by a vengeful spirit, became caught and tore with a dramatic "RIIIIIP!" The iron stair sneered, "Another victim claimed!"

Terrified, Alex stuffed the now-tattered cloak into a nearby trash can, assuming it would never be seen again. The cloak, now mingling with banana peels and old math homework, thought, "If I'd known I'd end up here, I'd have stayed in the wardrobe."

Alex scurried back to the changing room and snatched a new cloak. When Brandon, the so-called star of the show, arrived, he found the cloak bin empty. The only star he was now, was "Cloakless Brandon." His friends erupted in laughter, calling him names like "Brandon the Bare" and "Baron von No-Cloak."

But wait! Ryan, the class MacGyver, came to the rescue. With the heart of a saint and the fashion sense of a sleep-deprived artist, he offered his own cloak to Brandon. And then, with a glint in his eye, Ryan draped himself in a teacher's shawl, his makeshift cloak sagging under the weight of unflattering tassels.

"It's fashion-forward," he said, admiring his reflection in a spoon.

Still not satisfied, Ryan eyed the tablecloths. After an epic battle with a stubborn knot and some embarrassing attempts at draping, he crafted a makeshift cloak, complete with a shiny strip on the edges and a teacher's collar pin as a clasp. It was as fancy as a dining room table at a medieval feast!

The teacher, oblivious to the backstage drama, entered and asked if the kids were ready. The children's excited chorus of "We're ready!" echoed in the room. Brandon, grateful yet also a little afraid of Ryan's sartorial choices, offered to swap, but Ryan refused, declaring, "I've worn weirder things on a Tuesday."

Upon seeing Ryan's unconventional attire, Brandon recommended Ryan for the final dance, hoping the teacher's love for creativity would trump his apparent lack of coordination. Surprisingly, she agreed!

During the performance, Ryan's dance was nothing short of legendary. A blend of interpretive dance, accidental acrobatics, and vigorous tablecloth twirling, it left the audience both confused and mesmerized.

After the show, when questioned by Brandon's puzzled parents, Ryan simply said he applied the ACS" Rule: Assist, Create, and Stumble Around Gracelessly... uh, Shine!" Laughter and hugs were exchanged, and even Alex's cloak was forgiven for its betrayal.

They all left, content with their night of accidental triumph, gleefully pondering the moral that "everything happens for a reason," even if that reason is just stumbling into success with a tablecloth and a dream.

Study Questions

1. How did Alex handle the situation of tearing his cloak and taking a second cloak without permission?
2. What impact did Brandon's missing cloak have on his role in the end-of-year performance, and how did Ryan help him?
3. What problem-solving skills did Ryan demonstrate in creating a new cloak from a tablecloth and a collar pin?
4. What lesson can be learned from Ryan's application of the ACS rule, and how can it be applied in other situations?
5. How did the characters' attitudes towards the situation affect the outcome of the performance?
6. How could the situation have been avoided if the students were more careful with their cloaks and communicated better about the availability of spare cloaks?
7. How did the characters' experiences with the lost cloak contribute to their personal growth and development?

Guide to Creativity and Problem Solving

Human creativity involves the process of combining and connecting various materials to solve problems or take advantage of opportunities. In other words, creativity is about using what already exists to make something new and functional.

While there may seem to be only one way to accomplish a task, there can actually be hundreds of different solutions. What's essential is for individuals to develop themselves and expand their ability to identify these options. In many cases, creativity emerges as a way of linking problems with the objects in our surroundings.

For instance, attempting to put out a fire with a car might lead to the discovery of a fire engine. It's also intriguing how pocket watches were once carried around, until someone came up with the idea of attaching them to their wrist, resulting in the invention of wristwatches.

A critical prerequisite for being creative is to have faith that there can be a creative solution to any problem, and that we can find it. Someone who doesn't believe in creative solutions will never explore such options.

On the other hand, someone who believes that a creative solution can always be found will derive pleasure from solving problems. They will engage their brain to find solutions, and the various paths they discover along the way will give them joy.

At its core, creativity involves the ability to connect objects and concepts in a way that addresses a problem and yields a solution.

One of the most essential elements of creativity is the ability to see beyond the immediate problem or challenge, and to look for connections and relationships between seemingly disparate things. This requires the cultivation of a flexible mindset that can break down barriers and identify unexpected solutions.

Furthermore, creativity often involves taking risks and being willing to make mistakes. In order to come up with new and innovative ideas, it's important to be comfortable with uncertainty and ambiguity, and to be willing to explore multiple paths until you find the right one. This can require a certain level of courage, as well as a willingness to fail and learn from mistakes.

The process of being creative can also be highly rewarding and enjoyable. When we engage in creative problem solving, we activate the reward centers in our brain and experience a sense of pleasure and satisfaction. This can help to boost our confidence and self-esteem, and can also improve our overall well-being and mental health.

In addition, creativity can be highly contagious, and can inspire others to think more creatively and come up with their own innovative solutions. When we share our ideas and collaborate with others, we can create a synergistic effect that leads to even greater creativity and innovation.

Overall, the ability to be creative is a vital skill in today's rapidly changing world. By cultivating a mindset of flexibility, risk-taking, and openness, we can unlock our full creative potential and make a positive impact on the world around us.

Chapter 2 Being Solution Oriented

Soccer Game

John loved playing soccer and would play during every break at school. However, the breaks were too short, and when he went home, his mother wouldn't allow him to play with his friends. Occasionally, on some weekends, his family would let him play indoor soccer.

One Saturday, John asked his mother for permission to play soccer again, but she said the family was going to visit relatives. John felt helpless and started thinking of ways to play more soccer. Suddenly, he had a good idea.

When he went to school on Monday, John went to the principal's office during the first break. He said to the principal, "Sir, teamwork and collaboration are very important everywhere. I have a project to develop teamwork and collaboration in our school. If we organize an inter-class tournament, each class can bond and develop a team spirit. Additionally, we can appoint a teacher to coach each team, which would create a stronger bond between the teacher and the students."

The principal responded, "That's a great idea. I love basketball, so let's organize a basketball tournament." John was shocked and said, "Sir, we need tall people for basketball. There aren't enough tall people in each class to form a team. If we organize a soccer tournament, everyone can participate easily." The principal said he would think about it and sent John on his way.

The next day, when John came to school, there was a poster for a soccer tournament on the entrance gate. John was filled with unspeakable joy.

All the classes began practicing, and each teacher made selections. Everyone had to shoot at the goal, and those who scored at least one of their two shots made the team. John had bad luck and failed to score on his first two attempts. He couldn't join the team. Sadly watching the others, the teacher announced that the team didn't have enough players. Those who failed to score were given two more chances to shoot. John scored two goals in his second attempt and was finally able to join his class's team.

John's class teachers were very involved with the team. They scheduled practices for both after school and on weekends. John now had plenty of time to play soccer and was very happy.

His parents now allowed him to attend soccer practices. Time passed, and the tournaments began. Matches were played at school for a week. The final two teams were scheduled to play a final match on the weekend, and one of them would win the school cup. John's class was one of the two teams in the final.

The game began with great excitement, and both the players and the spectators were very anxious. In the first half, the opposing team scored three goals against John's class, who failed to score a single goal. In the second half, John's team quickly advanced to the other side of the field. The ball came to John's feet very close to the goal, and he scored the first goal. As the game approached the final five minutes, John scored his second goal and also the second goal for his team. At that moment, his family was very proud of him. In the last minute of extra time, the ball came to John's feet again. He kicked it so hard that his shoe came off. First, his shoe hit the goalpost, then the ball went into the net. It was probably the first time in soccer history that such a thing had happened. The referee said a foreign object first entered the goal and didn't count the goal. As much as they protested, the goal wasn't counted, and their team lost.

John returned home feeling sad. His parents were discussing his love for soccer in the living room, and then they called John in and told him that they would send him to a soccer summer school.

John received the best news of his life, and he was overjoyed. He couldn't contain his excitement and almost jumped to the ceiling in the middle of the living room. His little brother watched in amazement as their parents' attitude toward John changed drastically. Curious, he asked, "How did you manage to get into a soccer summer school?"

John replied, "My goal was to play soccer, but since our parents didn't allow it, I had two choices: give up or find a way to solve the problem. I could have played in secret, but that would have just avoided the problem. Instead, I decided to tackle the problem head-on. I faced some obstacles along the way, but I didn't give up. I remained focused on finding a solution.

Study Questions

1. What was John's initial problem regarding playing soccer, and how did he feel about it?
2. What was John's idea for developing teamwork and collaboration in his school?
3. How did John respond to the principal's suggestion to organize a basketball tournament instead of a soccer tournament?
4. How did John come up with the idea of organizing a soccer tournament at school?
5. What did John do when he failed to score on his first two attempts during the selection process for the soccer team?
6. What happened during the final soccer match, and how did John react to the outcome?
7. How did John's determination to play soccer despite his parents' disapproval ultimately pay off?

Guide to Being solution oriented

Problem, or in other words, an obstacle that prevents us from achieving our goals. When people encounter a problem, they show different approaches.

Some people get used to living with the problem instead of trying to solve it. For instance, Kerri, a hardworking student, faces a bully named Kevin, who is larger than him, and demands that Kerri give him answers during every exam. Kerri doesn't want to give in, but he does so anyway. After a while, this situation becomes a habit. If he gets caught providing Kevin with answers, Kerri's exam will be canceled, but he can't stand up to Kevin or tell the teacher that Kevin is forcing him to cheat. Instead of focusing on solving the problem, he gives up and lives with the problem without doing anything.

One of the main behaviors people exhibit when facing problems is complaining about the problem without taking any action to solve it. For example, a child who complains about the difficulty of math doesn't do anything to make math easier. If you work on something that is difficult, it becomes easier. However, continuing to complain does not solve the problem.

Some people delegate the solution to someone else rather than solving the problem themselves. A child who doesn't want to do their term project may have a friend or sibling do it for them. But if they were subjected to an oral exam about the project, they wouldn't be able to answer any of the questions.

Another approach to problems is to cover them up or in other words, to say "no, there is no such problem." In this way, an existing problem is hidden, and no steps are taken to find a solution. For instance, a student who struggles to learn a foreign language can't find a solution without first acknowledging the problem. A special book, website, course, or another solution can be found after accepting the problem.

To solve a problem, it is necessary to identify the problem and decide to solve it. To solve the problem, you must work on it, pay a price, and consider different options for the solution. Someone who has no intention of solving the problem won't develop any options and won't be prepared to work to solve it. However, someone who is determined to solve the problem will develop options and try them one by one until they find the solution. They will continue to try without giving up until they solve the problem.

Those who are determined to eliminate the problem can find innovative solutions.

Chapter 3 Critical Thinking and Questioning

Lost Pencils

Emily lost her pencils every day at school. No matter how hard she tried, she never returned home without losing a pencil. Her mother was very angry about this situation. One day, Emily's mother gave her a pencil and said, "I expect you to take care of this pencil. If you lose it, I won't give you another one."

The next day, Emily went to school with the pencil hanging from her neck. She didn't lose her pencil until the end of the school day and happily returned home. However, on the way home, the knot of the string holding the pencil came undone, and the pencil fell. When Emily entered the house, she held the string and said, "Mom, look, I didn't lose my pencil today!" but there was no pencil on the end of the string. Emily said, "Mom, I hung the pencil on this string, but it fell off," and her mother replied, "Should I hang you with that string if you lose another pencil? You're driving me crazy, Emily!"

The next day, Emily found a new way to avoid losing her pencil. She divided the pencil her mother had given her into three pieces and even though she lost a piece of the pencil every day, she asked for a new pencil from her mother after three days. Her mother was surprised that Emily hadn't lost her pencil in three days and said, "Good for you. This time you asked for a pencil three days later."

To keep from losing her pencil, Emily decided to tie it to her notebook. But she divided the pencil into three pieces again and tied one of the pieces to her notebook. However, during one of the breaks, she still managed to lose her pencil. This time, Emily asked herself a deeper question, "Why am I losing my pencils?" She thought it was strange that she kept losing pencils even though she was trying so hard to keep them. Maybe someone was stealing her pencils. If so, she had to catch the thief.

The next day, she dipped the remaining piece of the pencil into red paint and placed it on top of her desk. If someone took her pencil, their hands would be covered in red paint. During the break, she left the classroom and returned to find her pencil was gone. She reported the situation to her teacher and said, "You owe me a pencil." After listening to Emily's story, the teacher gave her a pencil as a gift.

The next day, Emily's classmate, Max, approached her with red paint on his hands. Emily asked, "Why did you take my pencils? Why?" Max said, Sure, here's a possible rewording of Murat's explanation:

"Ece, I'm sorry for taking your pencils without asking. I know it was wrong, and I shouldn't have done it. I was just jealous because you always had such nice pencils, and I wanted to have them too. I didn't realize that I was hurting you by taking them, and I didn't think about how it made you feel. I'm really sorry for what I did, and I promise I won't take your things without asking again."

Emily said, "Just don't do it again. I'm really tired of this situation."

When Emily returned home that evening, she told her mother what had happened. Her mother listened in surprise and said, "Well done! You really solved that problem!"

Emily continued, "Mom, at first, I focused on not losing my pencils. Then, I went to the root of the problem. I asked myself, 'What is causing me to lose my pencils?' When I found the root cause of the problem, I was able to solve it."

Her mother replied, "I'm sorry for getting mad at you. It wasn't your fault. I'll buy you a new box of pencils, my dear."

Emily said, "It's not necessary, Mom. Max promised to bring me a dozen pencils. I'll write this story with the first pencil I receive."

Signed, Emily

Study Questions:
1. What was Emily's initial reaction to losing her pencils every day?
2. Why did Emily's mother give her only one pencil and make her promise to take care of it?
3. What was Emily's strategy to avoid losing her pencil after she lost the first one hanging from her neck?
4. Why did Emily start suspecting someone was stealing her pencils?
5. What was Emily's plan to catch the thief who was taking her pencils?
6. Why did Max take Emily's pencils, and how did he feel when he got caught?
7. How did Emily solve the problem of losing her pencils, and what did she learn from the experience?

Guide to Critical Thinking and Questioning

Critical thinking is essential for individuals to innovate and create something new. As soon as a baby is born, the people raising it start teaching it everything they know about the world. The child learns the right and wrong things from parents or caregivers. When the child enters primary school, the teacher becomes the authority figure who teaches the child all the right information, which the child accepts as the only truth. As time passes, everything learned becomes an unquestionable fact. During the early years of primary school, children are particularly exposed to the importance of "memorization," such as memorizing the multiplication table, a poem, and so on. The better a child can memorize, the more they are perceived as smart and appreciated by their peers and teachers. However, one of the conditions of memorization is that children receive knowledge without questioning it.

A child who does not develop the ability to question what they are taught cannot step outside the box of preconceived knowledge and standard patterns of behavior. All the knowledge they are exposed to and all the ways of life they are shown are perceived as the only right ones, leaving no room for questioning. Children only question issues that affect their personal interests. For example, they might question why their playtime is being limited, why they cannot eat chips, or why they have to go to bed early and wake up early.

The fundamental tool of questioning is the question "Why?" Some children systematically try to discover the real logic behind everything by asking "Why?" to everything. When the question "Why?" is added to everything, people start to think. Why are 24 hours in a day divided into 10 hours instead of something else? Why do almost all people in the world like drinking tea? Why is inheritance distributed differently in different countries? Why do we drink cow's milk? Isn't cow's milk for calves? Why do they respect cows in India? Why aren't there three days off on weekends instead of two? Why do we go to school in winter, a time of better weather, instead of summer? Is it more important to sit down with someone or to chat? Why don't parents listen to their children? Why don't children listen to their parents? Why do we say there are 30 days in a month even though we use a solar calendar? Why are angular tables and desks dangerous, especially for babies and children, while home furnishings are not made with rounded edges? Why are we afraid of talking to new people? Why don't we read books?

Questioning has two basic elements:

What if it didn't exist? (What if there were no tables at home? What if there were no televisions? What if there were no textbooks? What if there were no pens?)
What if it did exist? (What if every kitchen had a fire extinguisher? What if small television screens were added to music sets? What if calendars were added to wall clocks? What if everyone had a cat?)
Asking "Why?" about almost anything takes us out of our normal mindset and helps us think about new alternatives.

Chapter 4 Developing Alternatives

Connecting Papers

Teacher Sarah entered the classroom with two blank sheets of paper in her hand. The students thought they were going to take a quiz, but the teacher showed them the papers and said, "Kids, we will work on today's lesson with these two papers and then we will all eat the three square cakes that I brought."

The students were surprised by what their teacher said, but they waited curiously. Teacher Sarah sat down at her desk and asked her question:

"How many different ways can we connect these two papers without using tape, a pin, a needle, glue, or wax?"

"I will take your answers according to a certain rule:
The first person to speak will offer one solution,
the second will offer two solutions,
the third will offer three solutions,
and the fourth will offer four solutions.
Everyone who speaks will bring one more solution than the person who spoke before.
Is that clear?"

The whole class nodded in agreement, and their teacher gave them two minutes to think.

First, John raised his hand and said, "We can use a stapler, teacher."

Lily gave a two-solution answer: "We can press the two papers together with a bobby pin," and "We can put play dough between the two papers."

Everyone loved Lily's solutions. When it was time for the third answer, the whole class anxiously waited to see who would raise their hand. Max raised his hand and said, "We can light a candle, let the hot liquid that accumulates on it drip onto one piece of paper, then place the other paper on top of it to stick them together. We can also cut the adhesive part of an envelope and use it like tape between the two papers. Another solution is to stick the two papers together with a chewed piece of gum."

It was time for the fourth answer, and everyone was very excited. They needed four more different solutions. For a long time, no one raised their hand, so Teacher Sarah said, "Okay, let's think a little more." At that moment, Alex said, "I found it," and raised his hand. Everyone started to listen to Alex with curiosity.

"First, we can take a piece of a sticker used in stores and stick the two papers together. Second, we can clamp the two papers with a clothespin. The third solution is to punch a hole on each side of the paper with a hole punch and tie them together with a string. Finally, we can sew the two papers together with a needle and thread."

The teacher congratulated Alex, and the whole class applauded him.

Just when everyone thought "There couldn't be more methods," Ethan raised his hand.

"We can connect the two papers with two magnets. We can use two toothpicks to connect the papers to each other like a needle. We can sandwich the two papers between two panes of glass to connect them to each other. We can attach the papers to each other with two interlocking Lego pieces. We can make a small hole in each paper, pass a bicycle chain through the holes, and connect the papers with the chain. We can sew one of the papers with a female snap fastener and the other with a male snap fastener and attach them."

The students were amazed and said things like "Wow, great." No one could have come up with more solutions than Emma, but then Tyler raised his hand.

We burn two handles of a plastic bag with a lighter, then quickly blow it out and stick the two papers together with the sticky liquid that has formed. The bag in between binds them.
We put two papers in between pages of a newspaper, and when they get squeezed, they become connected.

We place two speakers with one centimeter gap between them, turn up the music set to the maximum, and the papers stick together with the power of sound.

We park two cars bumper to bumper, and the papers get sandwiched between the bumpers.

We jam the two papers between two weights at the end of a barbell in the gym, and the papers become connected to each other.

Two people put their heads together. We place the papers between their heads. As long as their heads remain touching, the papers become connected to each other.

Everyone was amazed by the seven new methods that Tyler found. Even after a minute had passed, no one could come up with an eighth method.

Study Questions

1. If you were Teacher Sarah, what unique method would you suggest to connect the two papers without using tape, pins, or glue?
2. Can you think of any other everyday objects that could be repurposed creatively to join the two papers together?
3. How might you modify one of the existing solutions to make it even more efficient or innovative?
4. What other principles of physics or chemistry could be harnessed to connect the papers in an unconventional way?
5. Imagine you have access to a futuristic technology not mentioned in the story. How would you use it to connect the papers in a completely new and surprising manner?
6. Suppose you were given the challenge to connect three or more papers together using the same restrictions. How would you approach this problem creatively?
7. How might the methods proposed by the students be applied in real-world scenarios outside of just connecting papers? Can you think of any practical applications for these creative solutions?

Guide to Developing Alternatives

The phrase "Great minds think alike" is popular, but it can be misleading. While it's true that intelligent people can come to a sensible solution, there are often multiple ways to solve a problem that make sense.

Believing that there is only one reasonable solution is a mistake. Smart people can find many ways to solve a problem, while those with weaker minds may struggle to find a solution at all. Therefore, finding more than one solution is the rational way to approach a problem.

Having only one idea can be dangerous, especially if it turns out to be wrong. The evaluation of different ideas is key to finding the right one.

Consider the example of going to a store to buy a sweater. The seller says we can choose any sweater we want, but all of them are the same. With no differences between them, we have no real choice. True freedom requires options.

Without options or alternatives, we cannot be free. It is important to be creative and develop multiple solution alternatives to the problems in our lives. This is the function of a free mind. A person with a closed mind cannot think of new ideas or options.

To think of different paths, we must meet different people, have different experiences, and expose ourselves to new ideas. Traveling to unusual places, doing unusual sports, reading unusual books, and doing unusual jobs can all help open up our minds.

The mind is like a parachute; it only works when it's open. To keep an open mind, we must put prejudices aside and question generalizations. While having alternatives is key to finding solutions, we must also learn to be selective and evaluate each idea. With a mind that is accustomed to thinking with alternatives, we can find many ways out of every problem, and no one can stop a working mind.

Chapter 5 Constructive Criticism

Yellow Flower

I am writing this article for my composition class. Our teacher asked us to write about the story behind our own name. When my parents were expecting me, they started thinking about a name for me, but only ordinary names came to their minds. My grandmother insisted on giving me her own name, Susan. My mother, however, wanted a different name. She suggested, "Let's give her a flower name, like Tulip, Narcissus, Daisy, or Magnolia." My father said, "If we're going to do that, why not name her Chrysanthemum?" A friend of my father warned, "People live with their names. Having the word 'crisis' in your daughter's name will only create crises for you." My mother questioned this too, thinking that if she gave me a name like Magnolia or Daisy, it would be too ordinary. My grandmother loved yellow flowers, and my mother ultimately decided to name me after them, thinking that there was no such name as "Yellow Flower." However, this decision had unexpected effects on my life.

Yellow is an attention-grabbing color, and during the short time I have lived, it has led me to pay special attention to everything. Just as my mother critically examined ordinary names, I began to look critically at everything ordinary. Whenever I see something, I wonder why it couldn't be different.

When I was five years old, my friends were playing frisbee in the yard, but I wanted to play too, and I didn't have a frisbee. Frisbee is a round, flat plastic toy, usually yellow, that flies like a spinning disc when thrown. Although my parents did not buy me one when I asked, I thought, "Do I really need a frisbee to play this?" I realized that I could use the lid of the teapot instead, as it was similar to a frisbee and the perfect size for my small hands. One day, however, the lid fell into the sewer, and my mother was very upset. I thought for a moment and said, "If you're making tea, you already have a lid because you put the lid on the teapot. You don't need the lid when you're just boiling water, so I'll give you a nice lid that will not be found in the kitchen and will even let you know when the water boils." My mother was surprised. I quickly added, "Turn on the stove. I'll bring the lid from my room now." My mother put the teapot, full of water, on the stove, and I brought my flower-patterned bouncing ball with a bell inside from my room. My mother looked at the ball and said, "Is this the lid?" I said, "Look, mom, when the water boils, the ball on top will jump up and down and make a sound. You'll know when the water is boiling. The only trick is not to turn the stove on too high, so the plastic ball won't get damaged by the heat."

My dad used to love watching the news, but I couldn't understand why. He was always interested in important events, like when the president met with a European leader. But for me, that kind of news had nothing to do with us. And when a Dutch pilot won a Formula 1 race, I didn't care at all. The results only mattered to him and his team.

What we really needed was news that affected us, so I created a bulletin board to share stories about our family. I asked my dad what was happening at work, and he said he had attended a leadership training where he learned that leaders are rebellious. He also shared that he was likely to get a promotion in a month. My mom added that "even your dad doesn't know, but I think you're going to have a sibling." I also added that I was selected to represent the fourth-grade team in an upcoming debate competition.

That night, when my dad turned on the TV news, I had a surprise for him. I had rigged a string to the circuit breaker and turned off the power. When he went to get a candle, I put the bulletin board in front of the TV using a flashlight. When he came back, I told him I'd made a "family news" board while the power was out. He was astonished, especially when he read the third news story about my mom's surprise announcement. Once the TV news was over, I flipped the circuit breaker back on with the end of a broom and revealed the bulletin board to my parents.

I always approached everything critically. If there was a game, I would question why the rules were like that and if they could be different. I wondered why we had to sit in the same spots in class every day. And I asked if something bad happened, couldn't there be any good in that? At first, my classmates thought I complained about everything, but I was only trying to improve things.

In school, I realized that our break time was always the same, so I suggested to our classmate Betty, who was skilled in playing the piano, that she could record music to be played during our break time. Betty agreed, and when I proposed the idea to the principal, she was hesitant at first but eventually decided to give it a try. Break time then began with a recording of Betty's beautiful piano music, and once her piece was finished and the school became quiet, we knew it was time to return to class. The new break time music was a hit, and my classmates no longer complained about my tendency to think critically.

Study Questions
1. How did the main character's name, "Yellow Flower," make her always want to know more and find creative solutions to problems?
2. When she was five years old and wanted to play frisbee, how did she use her imagination to come up with a fun alternative to a real frisbee?
3. How did she surprise her parents by creating a special "family news" board and what was the news that amazed them?
4. How did the main character use her creative thinking to make break time at school more enjoyable for everyone?
5. Why did her classmates initially find her different, and how did they eventually come to appreciate her unique ideas?
6. Can you think of a time when you wondered why something was done a certain way and how you imagined a better solution?
7. Why is it important to be curious and think creatively, and how can it help you solve problems and come up with fun ideas in your daily life?

Guide to Constructive Criticism and Destructive Criticism: Understanding the Difference

Criticism is an essential aspect of growth and development. When we provide constructive criticism, we are offering feedback that helps improve a person or a situation. On the other hand, destructive criticism tears down and belittles a person, a situation, or a thing. In this essay, we will explore the difference between constructive criticism and destructive criticism.

Constructive criticism is a gift that can lead to progress and growth. It highlights specific areas that require improvement and offers suggestions for how to make improvements. The purpose of constructive criticism is to help individuals grow and develop. It aims to provide feedback that is beneficial and supportive, with the intention of improving future performance.

For instance, if an employee has made a mistake at work, constructive criticism would be to explain what went wrong and how the employee can avoid making the same mistake in the future. This kind of feedback helps the employee to learn and grow, and ultimately leads to better performance.

Destructive criticism, on the other hand, aims to tear down and belittle the person or situation being criticized. Destructive criticism is not helpful, and it does not provide any specific feedback that can lead to improvement. Instead, it is intended to harm the person or situation being criticized, without offering any suggestions for how to make things better.

For example, if a student receives a poor grade on an assignment, destructive criticism would be to say, "You are stupid and incapable of learning." This kind of feedback is not helpful and is intended to cause harm, without offering any suggestions for improvement.

It is important to understand that criticism can be both constructive and destructive, depending on how it is delivered. A critique that is delivered in a hostile or negative manner can be destructive, even if the feedback is technically constructive. For instance, if an employer provides feedback in a condescending or belittling manner, the criticism becomes destructive.

In conclusion, constructive criticism is an essential aspect of growth and development. It is intended to help individuals improve and develop, and it provides specific feedback that can lead to progress. Destructive criticism, on the other hand, is not helpful and can cause harm. It does not provide any specific feedback that can lead to improvement, and it is intended to tear down and belittle. To ensure that criticism is constructive, it must be delivered in a supportive and helpful manner, with the intention of improving future performance.

Chapter 6 Logical Reasoning

How Do I Get to School?

When Jerry woke up and checked the time, he freaked out. He was running late, and he had missed the school bus. How was he going to make it to school on time? He quickly brainstormed a solution in bed and went straight to his mom: "Mom, they make a killer sandwich in our school cafeteria; we always have breakfast at home. If you're down, you can drop me off at school, and we can have breakfast together there." His mom agreed, and Jerry made it to school on time. That day, his teacher asked, "Could your dad pay me a visit sometime?"

The next day, Jerry was late again and had missed the bus. This time, he went to his dad and said, "Dad, our teacher invited you to school to have a chat. We can go together today, and you can drop me off at school. We both get to meet the teacher." His dad was onboard with the plan, and they went to school together. Jerry made it to school on time.

On the third day, Jerry was in shock when he looked at the time. He had overslept by half an hour, and the bus had already left. Most likely, his parents had left the house too. He quickly got dressed and thought of a solution. Finally, he came up with a brilliant idea. He would wait at the entrance of the apartment building and ask the neighbors who came out, "Are you going in the direction of our school?" If he found a neighbor going in the same direction, he would go with them to school. He executed his plan flawlessly.

He caught John, Emily, Olivia, Robert, and Samantha as they left the building, but none of them were headed in the direction of the school. He was about to give up hope when Michael appeared from the elevator. He stopped and immediately asked, "Michael, do you pass by our school?" "Sure, Jerry," he replied. "I missed the bus today. Can I tag along with you?" "Absolutely." Jerry made it to school on time that day too, although they entered the classroom with the teacher.

On the fourth day, Jerry woke up when there were only ten minutes left before school started. Neither a private car nor a taxi could get Jerry to school on time at this point. Jerry got dressed quickly and headed towards the hospital across the street. He was praying as he walked. "I hope they get a call and pick up a patient from near our school." When he approached the ambulance, the driver rushed to the ambulance. Jerry shouted, "Are you going to Lincoln High School?" The driver replied, "How do you know that? I'm going to pick up the vice principal who is having a heart attack." "I'm coming with you," said Jerry. He miraculously made it to school again.

On the fifth day, when Jerry woke up, it was already past nine, and even an ambulance couldn't get him to school on time. He got dressed calmly, went outside, got on the bus, and arrived at his school around 10 am. He received a late slip from one of the vice principals and went into the classroom. Both the vice principal and the teacher scolded Jerry.

On the bus ride home, Jerry reflected on the adventures he had for the past five days. He had found an alternative way to get to school every morning, but he was stressed every morning, and on the last morning, he couldn't find a solution and was late for school.
As Jerry rode the bus home, a self-reflective inner dialogue emerged:

"Why am I always running late?
Because I oversleep.
Why do I oversleep?
Because I don't get enough rest.
Why can't I get enough rest?
Because I stay up too late.
Why do I stay up so late?
Because I get sucked into watching TV.
Why do I get sucked in?
Honestly, I'm not sure. Maybe it's just a habit.
Can I break this habit?
Absolutely, I control my actions.
From now on, no more TV for me.
There was no TV before 1950, why not try life without it?
TV has made me and so many others lethargic, but I've finally awakened."

Ozan refrained from watching TV over the weekend. On Monday, he woke up early, read some books, and made breakfast for his parents. His mother asked, "What's the occasion, son? You're up early today." Ozan responded, "I'm not a morning person, mom. I've just awakened.

Study Questions:

How did Jerry come up with the solution of having breakfast at school and getting a ride from his mom?

What was the significance of the teacher's request for Jerry's dad to visit the school?

What is the logic behind Jerry's plan of asking his neighbors for a ride to school on the third day?

What logical reasoning did Jerry use to ask the ambulance driver for a ride to school on the fourth day?

What logical steps did Jerry take to self-reflect and identify the root cause of his lateness and lack of rest?

What evidence does Jerry provide to support his decision to stop watching TV to break the habit of staying up too late?

How does Ozan's decision to refrain from watching TV on the weekend demonstrate logical reasoning and self-control?

13. Logical reasoning   Logical reasoning is the process of understanding the reasons behind an event or phenomenon. Everything that happens has a cause, and understanding the cause is the key to solving problems.

Problem-solving is a critical skill in all areas of life, and one essential aspect of it is identifying the root cause of the problem. This process requires logical thinking and careful analysis. To achieve a viable solution, one must not only address the symptoms of the problem but also identify and eliminate the underlying causes.

For instance, the water in a tea kettle boils due to the heat generated by the stove. In contrast, our feeling of coldness is due to the air's low temperature. Likewise, a student's poor exam results could be due to inadequate preparation. Every problem has a cause, and identifying the source is the first step towards a successful resolution.

One way to identify the root cause of a problem is to ask a series of "why" questions. For example, if a child wakes up late, we could ask, "Why did they wake up late?" The answer might be that they stayed up late watching their favorite TV program. So, the next question would be, "Why did they stay up late?" The answer could be that their favorite celebrity was a guest on the show. By continuing this process, we can trace the problem's root cause and find an effective solution.

Another essential step in problem-solving is taking action to address the root cause. For instance, if a high water bill indicates a leak, the problem will not resolve by merely paying the bill. Instead, we must find and repair the leak to prevent future charges.

In conclusion, a logical approach to problem-solving involves identifying the root cause of the issue, breaking down the problem through a series of "why" questions, and taking action to eliminate the cause. This methodology applies to all problems, from minor issues to more complex ones. By using a logical approach, one can effectively solve problems and make better decisions.

Chapter 7 Solving problems using information instead of violence

Bully's Redemption

Alex, a high school senior, had to make the final payment for his cell phone that day but had misplaced the money. He didn't want to ask his parents for more money, and if he didn't pay, he would have to return the phone. As he worried, an idea crossed his mind: "I'll bully a younger student and take his money," he thought and decided to target Jerry, who was not as physically strong. After school, Alex confronted Jerry and demanded, "Give me all the money in your pocket." But Jerry didn't have any money. He explained that he didn't get an allowance and Alex raised his hand as if to hit him, threatening, "You better figure out a way to get 50 bucks by tomorrow. If you tell anyone, I'll make sure you regret it."

"Do whatever you have to do to get 50 bucks tomorrow. If you complain to the teachers, the principal, or your parents about me, I'll ruin you." The next day after school, Alex approached Jerry again and asked, "Is the money ready?" Jerry replied, "I told you I don't get any allowance. I don't have any money. My family is having financial difficulties, and they won't give me that much money." Alex said, "I know what I'm going to do to you. You're going to be embarrassed in front of the whole neighborhood. If you complain to anyone, consider yourself dead. You'll go home in your undershirt now. Take off your jacket shirt." Jerry gave him his jacket and shirt. "Now you're going home like this. If you don't want to be even more embarrassed, you'll bring me the money tomorrow."

As Jerry walked away, a store owner who saw two boys pushing and shoving came to Jerry's side after Alex left. He quickly asked, "What happened, son? Why did you give him your jacket and shirt?" Jerry said, "He's trying to force me to give him money. He threatened me yesterday. Now, because I didn't give him the money, he's trying to embarrass me." The store owner said, "I sell clothes. Don't wander around like that. Let me give you a shirt." While Jerry was putting on his new shirt, the store owner said, "Knowledge and communication are the keys to solving problems." Jerry asked, "What do you mean? How can I get rid of this guy, Alex?" The store owner replied, "With knowledge and communication..."

Jerry thought about how he could solve the problem with knowledge and communication. He couldn't talk to Alex as he might still use violence against him. There had to be a way to protect himself from Alex's violence and help him. Jerry decided to write a letter to Alex. He would give the letter to his girlfriend to deliver to Alex in an envelope so that he wouldn't have to face Alex directly.

Jerry wrote the following letter:

"Dear Alex,

I can't say that I'm happy to have met you. But from what I've seen, you need help. Since you're forcing me to give you money, you must really need it, and you can't find another way to get it.

My folks aren't rich; they bought a new home and have got a ton of debt. They're frugal, so I don't get an allowance. I bring a sandwich from home every day to avoid buying at school.

But I want to lend you a hand. Let's figure out a rational and normal way to come up with the $50 you need. It's not cool for you to snatch cash from a little kid, me, or anyone else by using force. You wouldn't be stoked if someone bigger and tougher tried to pull that on you.

If you're down, let's meet up in the cafe during the last period today. You can spill your situation, and we'll brainstorm how to resolve your problem.

I'll catch you in the cafe during the last break.
Jerry

When Alex read Jerry's letter, he was both surprised and embarrassed. The child he tried to forcefully take money from wanted to help him. When they met at the canteen that day, the first thing Alex did was to apologize to Jerry. He then explained his situation, how he had to make a final payment for his phone in a few days but had dropped the money and couldn't ask his parents for more.

Jerry suggested, "The best way to make money is to work or trade. You can work at a store or try selling an unused game console or similar device you have at home."

Alex responded, "Work? It never crossed my mind. Even if I worked, they'd pay me a week later. But I do have an unused game console at home. But who can I sell it to?"

Jerry offered, "Let's put an ad on the school bulletin board, and an e-commerce site on the internet. My brother can help with the internet stuff." The next day, Alex brought Jerry's jacket and shirt.

Within two days, a student from their own school expressed interest in the game console, and Alex earned $100 from the transaction. Alex paid off his debt first and then treated Jerry to both dinner and a movie.

Study Questions

How did Jerry's critical thinking and problem-solving skills enable him to navigate a difficult situation with Alex?

In what ways did the store owner's advice about knowledge and communication help Jerry approach the problem with Alex differently?

How did Jerry's letter to Alex demonstrate empathy and a willingness to help, even after facing intimidation?

Reflect on a time when you faced a challenge or conflict with someone. How might you apply the lessons from Jerry's approach to resolving issues peacefully?

What alternative solutions could Alex have considered before resorting to bullying Jerry for money? How might these choices have affected the outcome?

How did Jerry's action of suggesting ways for Alex to earn money through work or trade demonstrate resourcefulness and creativity in problem-solving?

Imagine you were in Jerry's position, and someone approached you with a similar demand. What steps would you take to protect yourself while also helping the other person find a better solution to their problem?

Guide to Solving problems using information

In a world where violence and aggression have become commonplace, it is essential to remind ourselves that there are more intelligent and effective ways to solve problems. One such way is using knowledge and information, rather than brute force and aggression.

While there may be many ways to solve a problem, using violence is often the least intelligent and effective solution. There are numerous examples where problems cannot be solved through violence. For instance, if two siblings are unable to share a bicycle, physically fighting over it may result in the stronger sibling taking the bicycle, but it will also create a lasting animosity between the two. Instead, they could use the bicycle in a shared manner. If they both need it at the same time, one could offer to let the other use it, thus promoting understanding and cooperation.

Similarly, in a factory, if a machine breaks down, attempting to repair it without success may lead to frustration and anger. However, calling in an expert to fix the machine could lead to its repair, as the expert may possess the required knowledge and experience to repair it. Although the expert may charge a higher fee, their specialized knowledge is valuable, and paying for their services is reasonable.

To solve a problem, one should identify and define the problem before doing anything else. Instead of resorting to violence or yelling, one can explore various research avenues to find the solution. For instance, parents who complain about their child's behavior rarely try to find relevant information or read books on child-rearing techniques. Instead, they should research and seek out information about the topic. This information could include attending parenting classes, consulting professionals, or seeking advice from fellow parents. By taking such steps, parents can better understand their child's behavior and respond appropriately.

It is worth noting that problems can be resolved by using knowledge effectively. However, most people do not search for information when they face problems. While they may be willing to research a new place to visit or a new recipe to cook, they do not tend to research a problem they have with a friend or relative. In such cases, individuals tend to rely on themselves, which can lead to shouting or, in some cases, violence.

To conclude, the most effective way to solve problems is to acquire the necessary knowledge and use it effectively. Individuals must explore and seek information to resolve problems in the best possible way, avoiding the use of violence and aggression. By using knowledge as a tool, people can solve their problems without creating new ones.

Chapter 8 Being Independent

Courage to be a Lone Wolf

Mei, Jin, and Lin were three close friends who lived close to each other. They spent almost all their time together - going to school, playing games, and hanging out with their families on the weekends. One day, while coming back from school, Mei saw a flyer advertising a free violin course organized by the city. Excited by the opportunity to learn a new skill, Mei asked her friends if they wanted to join her. However, Jin and Lin were not interested. Jin found the sound of the violin unbearable, while Lin thought it would be too hard to learn and that nobody liked violin music anyway.

Despite her friends' lack of enthusiasm, Mei decided to go to the violin course alone. It was the first time she was separating from her friends, but she was determined to try something new. When she told her family about the free course and her desire to learn, they were surprised but supportive. Her family suggested she attend the first class to see if she liked it before committing to more lessons.

Mei went to her first class on a Saturday, and she was the only student who showed up. When the teacher learned that Mei did not have a violin, he told her she needed to purchase one. Mei asked her family to buy her a violin, but her father was hesitant. He was worried that she might lose interest in the violin and they would be left with a useless instrument. Despite her family's reservations, Mei continued to attend the class and asked her teacher if she could borrow a violin. The teacher contacted a former student and was able to secure a violin for Mei.

As she began to practice, Mei faced new challenges. Her long nails, which she was proud of, had to be trimmed to play the violin. The screechy sounds produced by the beginner's bowing were also not pleasant to hear. She had to practice for an hour each day, but the sound of the violin was disturbing to both her family and neighbors, and they asked her dad to stop her from playing. Her father scolded her for embarrassing the family and told her to give up the violin.

Mei brought up the issue of where to practice her violin with her teacher in their apartment building. The teacher suggested she could use the music room at the City's Community Activity Center. With daily practice and good guidance, Mei's violin skills continued to improve every week. After 32 weeks, Mei reached the level of a conservatory student and could play beautiful pieces that were pleasing to the ear.

One Monday morning, the school principal asked the teacher in charge to reach out to anyone who could contribute to the end-of-year show. Mei put herself forward to give a mini concert with her violin at the end-of-year show.

The last event of the end-of-year show was a concert, and as all the students were eagerly anticipating what would happen, Mei confidently appeared on stage with her violin and greeted everyone. Jin and Lin, who had no prior knowledge of this, were very surprised, and their families were watching Mei with great amazement. Mei gave an exceptional concert of seven pieces, which included popular selections from Beatles, Mozart, Sezen Aksu, and Star Wars, and played them flawlessly. At the conclusion of the concert, the audience gave Mei a well-deserved standing ovation.

After the show, Jin and Lin approached Mei and offered their congratulations, and asked her how she managed to achieve this level of excellence.

Mei replied, "If I hadn't taken the initiative to act independently from you at the beginning, I wouldn't have developed this skill, nor would I have had the opportunity to perform in this concert. They say that "the lone wolf dies, but the pack survives", but sometimes, it is the opposite, lone wolf thrives and the pack."

Study Questions

1. What motivated Mei to pursue the violin course despite her friends' lack of interest?
2. How did Mei's family initially react to her interest in learning the violin, and how did their support change over time?
3. What challenges did Mei face while learning the violin, and how did she overcome them?
4. How did Mei's determination to practice and improve her violin skills lead to an opportunity to perform at the end-of-year show?
5. Reflect on a time when you had to make a decision to pursue something independently, even if your friends were not interested. What were the outcomes of that decision?
6. How did Mei's persistence and dedication to learning the violin influence her friends, Jin and Lin, in the end?
7. What life lessons can be learned from Mei's journey, and how might her experience inspire others to explore new opportunities and follow their passions?

Guide to Being Independent

Independence is the foundation for building a distinct and personalized life and the ability to think differently. A person who can think independently has the capability to evaluate situations objectively and impartially and make rational and unbiased conclusions.

For instance, a football fan watches their team's game and evaluates every development from their team's perspective, whereas a non-fan watches the same match objectively and assesses the game of each team separately.

To be true to oneself, one must break free from negative and stereotypical influences of others. Every action must be made of one's own free will. For example, just because everyone is watching a popular television series, one should not feel obligated to do so. The individual should question whether they genuinely want to watch the series, and only then can they be independent.

Those who are incapable of thinking independently tend to act like a herd and imitate the behavior of the group they belong to. When listening to heavy metal music, one should be able to question whether they genuinely enjoy this genre or not. However, many are too afraid of being excluded from their group to ask this question, so they continue to listen to heavy metal music, whether they genuinely enjoy it or not.

Independent thinking requires new and different experiences. Therefore, an independent person is likely to make choices that suit their personal preferences while reading a book or planning a vacation. They will spend their time objectively and rationally, in a way that benefits them the most. Such a lifestyle ultimately enables a person to produce something unique and different from others.

Being independent does not mean being rebellious or disregarding the feelings of others. Freedom has limits, and one's freedom ends where another person's freedom begins. While being free to think and act, one should still consider the well-being of their loved ones. Making independent choices is essential while choosing a career instead of following the expectations of others.

An independent person is a unique individual and not a carbon copy of anyone else. They are not susceptible to the pressures or influences of others. Independence means that a person can think and make decisions on their own without being affected by the opinions of others. It enables a person to be self-sufficient and self-reliant, creating a life that is truly their own.

Chapter 9 Power of Humor

Fish Tales

Mel and his father returned from a fishing trip on Saturday, and when Mel entered the kitchen, his mother asked, "How'd it go? No fish?" Mel replied, "Are you kidding, Mom? We caught seven huge fish!" His mother asked about the fish, and Mel explained, "We were really lucky today. We caught seven big fish, but we only had enough money for my dad to take us to the lake. We didn't have enough for the trip back. So my dad asked the cab driver if he would take us if we gave him some of our catch. He agreed and drove us home for two fish. When we got home, we realized we left some of our fishing gear by the lake. We had to get back in the taxi, and we lost two more fish in the process. That's the story of our fish."
Mel's mother asked about the missing fish, and he responded, "As we were getting into the cab, a man approached us and said, 'Excuse me, my wallet was stolen. Can you spare some cash for the cab?' So my dad gave him one of the fish."

Mel and his father went fishing again on Sunday, but once again, they returned empty-handed. His mother said jokingly, "I guess the taxi driver's wife will cook fish tonight." Mel responded, "No, Mom. You won't believe what happened today." His mother asked, "Did you catch any fish?" Mel replied, "Of course we did, Mom. We caught a bunch! First, we caught a big fish, but we saw that it was blind in one eye. We didn't want to eat a fish like that, so we threw it back into the sea. Then we caught another fish, but it didn't have a fin. We couldn't eat a disabled fish like that, so we threw it back. The third fish we caught was even bigger than the first two, but it didn't have a tail. We had no choice but to throw it back too." His mother asked, "So you didn't catch any healthy fish?" Mel replied, "Of course we did, Mom. We caught 12 healthy fish." His mother asked, "Where are the fish then?" Mel said, "After catching those fish, my dad caught five big, healthy fish at once. We were about to pull them to the shore when a seagull swooped down and attacked our fish. More seagulls joined in, and before we knew it, they took all of our fish and flew away. They even pecked my dad's head." His mother asked, "Did they peck your tongue too, son?" Mel replied, "Why would they, Mom?" His mother joked, "Well, aren't you going in?" Mel replied, "Come on, Mom. Don't be funny. We had a tough day out there."

My dad was persistent and didn't give up. He fixed the fishing line and waited patiently to catch more fish. After some time, we felt some movement on the line. Dad started to reel it in, but suddenly the person fishing next to us started to reel in his line too. Our lines got tangled up, and they started arguing about whose fish it was. The other guy was bigger and intimidating. At the end, my father gave fish to him.

His mother asked curiously, "What's in that little box?" Mel replied, "Today was like magic, Mom." His mother was still puzzled and asked, "I don't understand how all these things happened, but what's in the box?" Mel explained, "Well, Mom, after all these incidents, we thought there must be a reason for all of it.
After Mel and his father returned home empty-handed from fishing, they decided to get creative. As Mel opened the box, his mother asked excitedly, "What's in the box?" Mel grinned and said, "You won't believe it, Mom. It's a tiny mermaid!" His mother's eyes widened in surprise and disbelief. Mel continued, "We caught her in our fishing net, and she begged us to set her free. But we said, 'No way, little mermaid, you're our lucky charm.' So we put her in the box and brought her home with us." His mother was both amused and skeptical, "Are you serious, Mel?" Mel replied, "Of course, Mom! We even gave her a name - Ariel. And now we're going to keep her as our pet and good luck charm." His mother chuckled and said, "Well, if she brings you good luck, then she's welcome here." Mel then pulled out a small glass bowl from the box and said, "And this is her new home." His mother looked at the bowl and asked, "But how can she live in there?" Mel replied, "We made her a tiny mermaid-sized house, complete with a little garden and everything." His mother shook her head, still not entirely convinced, but amused nonetheless. "Well, I never thought I'd have a mermaid for a pet," she said with a chuckle. "Just be sure to take good care of her." Mel grinned, "Don't worry, Mom. We're going to spoil her like a little princess." And with that, the family sat down to enjoy their day's catch, and the company of their new, tiny, fishy friend.

Study Questions:
What role does humor play in coping with failure in the story "Fish Tales"?

How does Mel and his father's creativity manifest in the story, and what role does it play in their success?

In what ways do Mel's responses to his mother's questions showcase his sense of humor in "Fish Tales"?

How does the humor in "Fish Tales" contribute to the overall tone and mood of the story?

How does Mel's mother respond to the different situations and the humor in "Fish Tales"?

How does the story "Fish Tales" explore the idea that creativity can come in different forms, even in everyday activities such as fishing?

In what ways does "Fish Tales" illustrate the power of humor and being funny in creating memorable experiences?

Guide to Power of Humor

Humor has the power to bring out the funny side of events in life. It is not only used to entertain or make people laugh but can also convey certain ideas.

For example, consider political satire such as The Daily Show or Saturday Night Live. They use humor to highlight current events, political commentary, and issues in society. This form of humor is not only entertaining but also raises awareness and provokes thought.

Various forms of content, such as speech, cartoons, stories, novels, comedies, puns, jokes, satires, and sarcasm, all have a common thread: the "joke". The "punchline" is a crucial element that is cleverly hidden within the details of the work. It is revealed at the right moment and unexpectedly, leading to laughter.

For instance, take the classic pun: "Why don't scientists trust atoms? Because they make up everything." This joke relies on the double meaning of the word "make up," which is unexpected and cleverly hidden within the sentence.

Humor, whether it be crude or delicate, is based on the sudden revelation of contradictions within the story.

Consider a classic example of a comedic contradiction in the movie Airplane! In the scene where the plane is crashing, one character yells "We're all gonna die!" while another responds "you can't be serious." The contradiction between the seriousness of the situation and the absurdity of the response is what makes this moment so funny.

Humor is a sophisticated and intelligent way of expressing creativity and problem-solving. Those who have mastered the art of humor are like talented spies or agents who can use it to get out of difficult situations.

One example of using humor to solve problems is the technique of "de-fusing" in conflict resolution. This technique involves using humor to lessen tension and make it easier to discuss difficult topics.

Furthermore, humor can be used to provide constructive criticism without hurting people. It can draw attention to a problem, rejuvenate a bored group, or even discuss a banned topic through humor.

Trevor Noah, former host of The Daily Show who is known for using humor to address important social issues. In one episode, he humorously highlighted the absurdity of the NCAA's policies on college athletes not being able to profit from their own image and likeness. His humor helped to draw attention to the issue and encouraged discussion and change. Another example is his use of satire to discuss politics and current events in a way that is both informative and entertaining, making the information more accessible and engaging to a wider audience.

Humor is a form of mental exercise. Creating humor requires a working mind, while listening, reading, or watching humorous content stimulates the mind. Humor is a showcase for creativity, entertaining people with quality jokes that contain a level of ingenuity similar to a stage show.

In summary, humor is a powerful tool that can entertain, provoke thought, solve problems, and even make difficult topics more approachable. Whether through satire, puns, or comedic contradictions, the use of humor requires creativity, intelligence, and an ability to see the funny side of life.

Chapter 10 Curiosity

White hair

Mateo was an inquisitive child with a never-ending stream of questions. He would always attempt to find answers himself, seek advice from loved ones, or scour encyclopedias and the internet for answers.

"Why are men's and women's clothing buttons sewn in different directions?" One morning, he asked his mother, "Mom, why are women's buttons on the left and men's on the right?" His mother was taken aback and responded, "I don't know, son. Perhaps it's to differentiate between men's and women's clothing." Mateo retorted, "But that can't be right, Mom. Men's and women's clothing is already vastly different. Dad's clothes wouldn't fit you, and yours wouldn't fit him. It's evident that they are designed for each gender. There must be another explanation." Mateo kept his query in mind and continued to ask adults, but no one knew the answer.

Women's buttons were stitched on the left side when buttons were first invented in the 17th century. Only the wealthy could afford dresses with buttons at that time, and they had servants who assisted with dressing. To make it easier for them, buttons were sewn on the left side of the garment, which matched the servant's right hand. On the other hand, men dressed themselves, so the buttons were sewn on the right side of their attire. Today, nobody employs servants to dress them, but clothing manufacturers still sew the buttons on the right side. What's more intriguing is that nobody ever questions why.

"Why are fuel tank caps on different sides of cars?" One day, Mateo went for a drive with his father, and they stopped at a gas station to fill up. The attendant requested, "Could you pull the car to the other side of the pump?" The fuel tank cap was on the left side of the vehicle, so it needed to be brought to the right side of the pump. Mateo queried, "Dad, why do some cars have fuel tank caps on the right side and others on the left? Are there male and female cars like the buttons sewn on the right or left?" His father explained, "In our country, cars drive on the right side of the road, while in England and some other countries, cars drive on the left side. When a car driving on the right side approaches a gas pump, the pump is on the right side, so it makes sense to put the fuel tank cap on the right side of the car. In countries like England, it's more logical to position the fuel tank cap on the left side." Nonetheless, even though all cars in the USA drive on the right side, fuel tank caps are located on both sides. Therefore, this explanation didn't answer Mateo's question. Gas pumps are situated in the middle of gas stations. If all fuel tank caps were on the right, all cars would have to face the same direction and queue up. However, because some car models have the fuel tank cap on the right and others on the left, some cars can park on the right side of the pump, while others can park on the left side.

"Why is the Day Divided into 12 Hours Instead of 10?"

One day, Mateo posed a question to his teacher, "Teacher, why is a day divided into 24 hours? Could it have been divided into 10 hours instead?" After considering the question, the teacher couldn't provide a satisfactory answer. Mateo decided to do some research on the topic and discovered some intriguing findings.

The day was divided into 12 hours because 12 is a more superior number in terms of divisibility than 10. For example, if we wanted to indicate a third of an hour, dividing the day into 10 parts would require expressing it as 3 hours, 33 minutes, 33 seconds, and 3.333333333333 milliseconds. The number 10 cannot be divided evenly by three.

However, the number 12 can be divided evenly by 2, 3, and 4. Similarly, the reason why an hour is 60 minutes rather than 100 minutes is because 60 can be divided evenly by itself, 2, 3, 4, 5, and 10. This enables us to use expressions like a quarter of an hour or 1/3 of an hour (20 minutes).

Mateo also pondered why the hands of a clock rotate clockwise. Through his research, he discovered that this was related to sundials. Sundials were mainly used in the northern hemisphere, and the shadow on the sundial moved in the direction we now call clockwise. When designing the mechanical clock, the formal structure of the sundial was replicated. Otherwise, the mechanical clock could have operated in the opposite direction.

"Why is Glass Transparent?"

Mateo was also curious about why glass is transparent. Glass is a solid object, yet it can transmit light. It was known that glass is made from sand, which is silicon. However, the sand on the beach doesn't appear to be transparent. Mateo's research led him to some fascinating discoveries.

The fact that glass transmits light is primarily due to the production process. Solid objects have tightly bound molecules, like bricks in a wall, that prevent their backsides from being seen. In contrast, the molecules of transparent liquids and gases, which also form a wall like bricks, are not tightly bound to each other. The molecules of liquids are more sparsely distributed, and the molecules of gases are even more sparsely distributed. This allows the backsides of liquids and gases to be seen.

When glass is produced, the sand we see on the beach is melted at high temperatures and transformed into a liquid. It is then cooled, and the glass we know is formed. The name given to the silicon dioxide that makes up glass is silica. The silicon dioxide doesn't contain the type of electrons that absorb light, which is why glass is a transparent object that transmits light.

Mateo's inquisitive nature and intriguing questions had made him well-known throughout the school. Even his teachers were often amazed by the questions he would ask and the answers he would find. An inter-school quiz competition was arranged, and the teachers decided to include Mateo in their team. Being the youngest member, Mateo was thrilled to be a part of the team. They performed exceptionally well, knocking out their opponents one by one, until they finally reached the finals, where they faced another formidable team. The competing school had always been the champion in the past, and no one gave Mateo's school a chance. As the inter-school quiz competition continued, the teams battled it out to answer a range of interesting questions. Mateo's team and their rivals were neck-and-neck until the final question was asked.

Earlier in the competition, Mateo's team was asked a question: "What is the largest organ in the human body?" Mateo's teammate quickly responded, "It is the skin!" and the team earned an extra point.

Meanwhile, during a tense moment in the competition, the rival school was asked, "What is the capital of Australia?" The rival team was quick to buzz in and one of them confidently answered, "Canberra." Because my father was born in Canberra. The host confirmed that it was indeed the correct answer.

As the final question was read, both teams were tied and knew that the correct answer would determine the champion. The host asked, "What is the name of the pigment that gives color to human hair?" Mateo's rival team looked stumped, but Mateo knew the answer. He said, "I want to explain the answer. Something that is not present in my father's hair is the answer to this question." His friends urged him eagerly, saying "Come on, tell us quickly!" Mateo said, "Okay, okay, the pigment that gives color to human hair is 'MELANIN'!" With this correct answer, Mateo's team won the competition and became champions.

Study Questions
1. How did Mateo's curiosity and drive to find answers influence his learning and education?
2. How did Mateo's teachers react to his curiosity and the unique questions he would ask?
3. How did Mateo's research skills contribute to his ability to find answers to his questions?
4. What can we learn from Mateo's experience in the inter-school quiz competition about the benefits of curiosity and learning?
5. In what ways did Mateo's questioning and research skills challenge conventional knowledge and understanding, as seen in his inquiries about clothing buttons and fuel tank caps?
6. How did Mateo's research on topics like the division of time and the transparency of glass change his understanding of these concepts and their importance in everyday life?
7. What strategies can be used to encourage and support children and students who have a strong sense of curiosity and a desire to learn more about the world around them?

Guide to Curiosity

Curiosity is a remarkable behavior that involves exploration, learning, and the pursuit of the unknown. It is a quality that has been observed in both humans and animals, from infancy to old age. Curiosity helps to drive progress in science and technology, as it inspires individuals to question the status quo and seek out new knowledge.

One of the defining characteristics of curious individuals is their tendency to ask spontaneous questions. They are constantly seeking to expand their knowledge and understanding of the world around them. Whether they are wondering why the moon is round or why most animals have a highly developed sense of magnetic direction while humans do not, curious individuals are always striving to uncover new information.

This pursuit of knowledge can be incredibly empowering. As their knowledge grows, curious individuals become more confident among others. They have a wider scope of knowledge and reach, and they often find themselves in a position to share their expertise with others. This, in turn, can lead to greater respect and admiration from those around them.

Curiosity can also help individuals develop their social skills. By asking questions of experts and people from different backgrounds, curious individuals can learn new perspectives and gain insights into the world around them. This can help them to build new relationships and expand their social circle.

Another benefit of curiosity is that it drives individuals to observe and seek understanding of what is happening around them. Curious individuals are always questioning why and how things occur and sometimes ponder who created them. They make comparisons to see the differences, and they often discover new insights as a result.

By constantly seeking answers to their questions, curious individuals can gain a deeper understanding of the world around them. They learn to look beyond the surface and explore the underlying causes and mechanisms that drive the world around them. This makes them better equipped to navigate the complexities of the world and to solve problems in new and innovative ways.

In conclusion, curiosity is a remarkable behavior that has helped to drive progress in science and technology throughout human history. It is a quality that inspires individuals to question the status quo, seek out new knowledge, and discover new insights. By cultivating our curiosity, we can expand our understanding of the world and empower ourselves to achieve great things.

Conclusion

As we come to the end of this enlightening journey through the realms of creativity, critical thinking, problem-solving, and the power of individuality, we stand at the threshold of transformation. Each chapter has been a key that unlocked the door to a world of endless possibilities and growth.

Through the enchanting stories of Lost Cloak, Soccer Game, Yellow Flower, and Fish Tales, we have witnessed characters grappling with challenges and embracing their unique strengths to find ingenious solutions. Alongside these captivating narratives, the study questions have sparked curiosity and provoked reflective thinking, inviting readers to delve deeper into the profound lessons each tale imparts.

The guide accompanying each chapter serves as a compass, pointing us in the direction of honing our creativity, becoming solution-oriented, nurturing critical thinking, and developing alternative perspectives. Through the exploration of constructive criticism and logical reasoning, we uncover the strength of communication and the immense potential of information in resolving conflicts without violence.

As we tread the path towards independence and embrace the power of humor, we discover the art of curiosity as the key to unlocking the hidden wonders of the world around us. In the tale of White Hair, we learn that asking the right questions leads to unearthing the most profound truths.

Dear reader, as you close this book, may the lessons within resonate in your heart and mind. May you carry forth the torch of creativity, wield the sword of critical thinking, and embrace the power of curiosity in your journey through life. Let the stories of these remarkable characters inspire you to be the solution-seeker, the independent thinker, and the harbinger of constructive change.

For in the tapestry of life, each thread represents a moment of transformation. Let this book be a testament to your unwavering commitment to growth, wisdom, and the unyielding pursuit of excellence. As you venture into the world, may you remember the lessons learned from these pages and embrace the endless possibilities that await you.

Your journey has just begun, and the world eagerly awaits the melody of your unique voice. So, stand tall, be bold, and let the symphony of your life be a testament to the power of creativity, curiosity, and the boundless potential that lies within you.

www.ingramcontent.com/pod-product-compliance
Lightning Source LLC
Chambersburg PA
CBHW030456010526
44118CB00011B/964